KATHLEEN SWANN

RIPPLES BEYOND THE POOL

First published in paperback format by
Coverstory books, 2019

ISBN 978-1-9993027-8-8

Copyright © Kathleen Swann 2019

Cover illustration "River Rothay" © Malcolm
Swann, 2019.

www.coverstorybooks.com

RIPPLES BEYOND THE POOL

KATHLEEN SWANN

Contents

Postcards

Fragments of History

Transformed

*

POSTCARDS

Circles

Low pressure is spiralling
a westerly carrying rain
drives the bore onwards
through the estuary
seabirds tack in the wind
against a sky of unpolished silver.

Salmon are finding their way
from deep ocean to the shallows
of their spawning grounds
mapping the journey   defying gravity
a final migration of procreation
against the run of time.

On this cool September evening
an old man stands smelling the air
feels the uneasy shift
of stones beneath his feet
as the river quickens
restoring the balance.

He takes long slow pulls of line
length by length   a measured
whip of gut in a figure of eight
slicing the dying light
the fly dances on the water
sends ripples beyond the pool.

Staffa Harp

The nose of a dolphin
breaks the waves of sound
from a resonating bird's wing
the prow of a boat
searches for the wind's breath
through a whispering sail.

Your wooden frame is warm
against my knees   my arms glide
my hands slip easily across
tight lines of gut and steel
ready for fingers to release
the music of your soul.

Bright notes lift me
to heights of volcanic cliffs
filled with young birds who wait
in the certainty that a parent
will return from beneath the sea
with fish for hungry mouths.

Bass tones cocoon me
in caves shaped by columns
of black basalt thrown from deep
within the earth long ago
a gaping mouth vibrates
with ancient Celtic song.

Song of the Tide on Walney Island

Sing of the dunlins
disguised in the shingle
riffling and prodding
their beaks in the sand
    the grey seals swim
on the rill of water
bobbing their heads
above waves in the wind.

Sing of the cattle
whose inherent instinct
brings them to safety
to graze on salt grass
    white crossed oyster-catchers
lined up in regiment
stabbing for food
backs to the tide.

Sing of the hills
rising in sunshine
look down on the town
the factories below
    windswept flowers
sea holly   horned poppy
sealed to the seashore
by salt-spit wind.

Piel Castle

There is a castle in the mist
  by the shore in the sea
   in the rain
a ragged shell calling
   to seals to waves
 to sea birds
   across incoming tide

raindrops prattle in my ear
  as cross-backed
   oyster catchers drift
  to land in the midst of the flock
screech fret wait
  beaks to the wind

rising tide fills rills and channels
  scatters waders
  to run search
   dip beaks
    in wakening mud
   shellfish move and open

eider swim in jostled huddles
  young ones trail
   in deepening surf
  greenshanks scurry
   bow and bustle
  gulls racing rising tide
pulled by a castle in the mist

Visitors to Nidderdale

Aware of your shadow beside me
wide hung wings and forked tail
slide over the valley side
eclipsing rocks
I shade my eyes to look
as you silently quarter the hillside.

Traffic packed roads and caravans
hold no terror for you as you glide
from river bank to rocky moor top
pale eyes search the ground
snatch your next scrap of flesh
from heather or sphagnum moss.

I watch as you rise on thermals
willing you to stay longer
allow me to share this silent hunt
in the turquoise light of sunset
but you turn   head south
primaries spread as you soar.

Suddenly I lose sight of you
a memory melting into cloud
I'm glad you are free
to hunt greensward and heath
I've seen the twisted bodies
of your kin.

Reflections on Coniston

Ribs of rock
  carved by ice
    gathering stones
      lakes and pools left
        by glacial water
          abandoned
            scooped out tarns
              gouged out gullies
                streams of water hurtling
                over green slate
                Arctic Char swim deep
                circling Bluebird for fifty years
              feeding, breeding, with no thought
            of death hidden beneath these waters

Swans
tails like
white sails
point to the sky
yachts sail by   tack
with the wind side to side
to catch a breath
          race shadows of clouds
          swing of the boom   air buffets the sail
          listing to starboard

Swallows

scoop mayfly

leave no ripples

skimmers swooping

kissing water moleskin wings twist and dip

make speed

summer

is

short

Limestone Wall

long white spine
travels upwards
with purpose
lurches over hilltops
tumbles into dips
unsteadily divides the land
through-stones tie wall to wall
bring strength   create stiles
for stouthearted walkers
rough stones nestle into each other
seeking a niche in a taciturn world
as mothered bodies hunker into a cubby hole
giving shoulder to the wind
blowing from the west
carrying the rain
that feeds the grass
lichen roses   powder moss
paint one side wintergreen
cap-stones
sit
like
teeth
across
the
top
biting at the wind
sheep take shelter on the leeward side
or pass through the sheep-creep
to graze on fresh fodder

rabbits disappear
squeeze through
impassable gaps whilst
the bone-white wall supports
them all

Jackdaws

Suddenly, like a fleet of F16s they land
feathers fill spaces, untidy balls of soot
squabble, siblings strut and preen
create havoc in the apple trees.

We watch from the kitchen as fruit plunges
to the ground, golden globes
peppered with holes from coal black beaks
as the autumn larder releases its harvest.

I wonder what they've been eating
through spring and summer
as they seek and greet their partners
with harsh dry barks and rooftop kisses.

Now that we've netted the chimney
who will leave a space for them to fill
with sticks, twigs, shiny plastic
to raise their chattering brood.

Winter will draw them from our mind
behind draped rooms we forget the call
of these scavengers cut from cloth of night
reminder of endurance.

Gannet

Snowy bodies
    with glacier eyes
land unsteadily on
    heavily populated cliffs.
Genus Morus
    the Solan Goose is
screeching   fighting
    in colonies
scrabbling ungainly
    on rafts of twigs
getting used to life
    on land again.

Beak sky-pointing
    says you will leave the nest
black tipped wingspan wide
    wheeling   turning   binocular vision
with the skill of the fletcher
    you retract your wings
dive from thirty feet
    air sacs like bubble wrap
protect your breast
    as you breech the water
sleek   streamlined
    fearless fishermen.

When the Robin Sings

Light is frozen, a rime of hoarfrost
spreads over upland to a hill
of wooden skeletons, stark, bare
standing in icy atmosphere.

Snowdrops, aconite, cyclamen
slowly emerge, seek protection
beneath leathery leaves
frost drops in silence.

Crisp white ice skims the pond,
captures grasses, reeds reach
for sun, wait to be released
by spring's slow return.

Daylight pulls at night's dark edges
shadows shrink in awakened warmth
winter turns his leaden back
and slinks away.

Chloe

In that quiet corner
I am melded to the wall forever
to watch the rotation of each year
decked in floral garlands
    in defiance of the gardener.

Spring twists fragrant clematis
around my studious head
delicate leaves   deep blue bells
I am a Greek goddess in full bloom
    as gentle rain rekindles life.

Midsummer winds pale roses round
my neck with thorns as sharp
as prickly heat   full sun saps colour
from the burgeoning border and I
    am hidden in aromatic bower.

Autumn has me decked in glorious hues
which cling defiantly to my bronze form
until sudden playful winds
peel my veils in slow seduction
    exposing my reality.

Winter's coat is bridal, softly drapes
every nook and crease, caresses
my hair with star white sequins
brought by the arctic fingers
    of a sharp north wind.

Summer's Leaving

In the hollow air is clean as
never breathed
autumn weighs heavy
on skeletons
of tall grasses
lays down spent stems
leaves flipped brown to silver
Burns Beck runs in rills
seamed into scrub land
soaks sphagnum moss
as branches bend
sipping from pools
that house frogs lizards
lily-pad stepping stones
where spiders sieve
the air for insects
tread softly
where green-streak
butterflies rest
take care not to trespass
on the flight path
of the tawny owl
as breezes draw a soft sigh
from leaves casting
silk-screen shadows
on our backs
follow the tracks of deer
through late summer reeds
overblown and overgrown

Scent

Unlike summer rain which falls quickly
dries in a hurry   leaves a smell of laid dust
the wash of damp autumn air
drifts in and out of late honeysuckle
sucks the musty smell from each gold trumpet
carries it   floating   over the borders
a spray of heady perfume
for bees gathering late nectar
I walk to the compost heap
where summers warmth has made
rich steaming loam with a dark aroma.

Graffiti

I sprawl languidly across the soot
               speckled wall   wait for people
  on the train to notice me.......

                  .....shake
    their heads in disapproval
  at such radical thoughts as these.....

   ....or laugh   uproariously
at the wit of the the artist
     who imagined me.........

   ......painstakingly shaped
          then coloured me
     voiced a protest
 in the dead of night
      by the light from a phone

Coventry

I am in awe of you
you make me humble
with your heart open for reconciliation

you have built your Cathedral
in such a way to remind the world
hate and revenge cannot bring peace.

I am transfixed by the engraved window
casting vernal images over old walls
contrasting beauty bridges ages

the crushing destruction is there
not to tend guilt or remorse
stoically shows what can grow from ruin.

I am in thrall to the meld
of modern glass and fabric
with a cross of bomb charred beams

as faces from across the globe
weave their lives through your structure
laughing, kissing, living a hopeful future.

I am brought to tears by optimism
in the room of paper cranes
created by a child of Hiroshima

to fly peace around the world
when she could not
I am silenced by your courage.

A Big Issue

She stands at the entrance
to the bustling arcade
a parcel of papers half hidden
by fake marble columns
as though they are shameful
not fit for respectable shoppers.

She pushes hobo gloves
back on her hands,
reveals long fingers decorated
with mendi scrolls, silver rings
an element of diversity
not generally seen in this town

Cardigan cuffs slide
from beneath coat sleeves,
woollen welts unravel
tight black jeans
emphasise skinny legs,
colour in her cheeks
from brusque rejection

People hurry past, canvas bags
filled with sugar laden treats
they catch sight of her
turn their heads as if
some interesting event
demands their attention.

Cold creeps up from her feet
she sinks lower into her coat
an island in a sea of people
her breath quickens
as papers disappear

bed and board secured
     -for one more night

Samba Cafe

How easily the women slip
into the men's arms
stranger or lover   locked
from rib-cage to thigh   swaying
to the beat of the boom-box samba
on the floor of the street cafe

How easily the young men
slide on and off the dance floor
change partners with a smile
learn a step   show a move
bewitch the audience   then
drift away into the lazy heat

How easily the old man
sheds the mantle of infirmity
clasps his partners hands and
with hypnotic lightness
rocks his shoulders   rolls his hips
claims the space for his sorcery

We sit and drink coffee
from white cups and saucers
tap our feet nonchalantly
to the rhythm   move our bodies
preparing to join the dance
but choose not to   just yet

Shibuya Tokyo

Pinball, pinball
>Slot machine, slot machine

Bagatelle, bagatelle

>*Pachinko*

Bright colours, shiny colours
>Metal pins, silver balls

Black heads bobbing

>*Pachinko*

Escalators rumbling
>Metal balls clattering

Japanese chattering

>*Pachinko*

First time, second time
>Tokens tumbling

Voices vibrato

>*Pachinko*

Casino, casino
>Temptation tugging.

Rent money dwindling

>*Pachinko*

Bar Piccolo

Heat sprawls over the Piazza Verdi
blurs walls of medieval buildings
grabs the colour from everything.
In the cramped reaches of the bar
half-recognised tunes chime
from an old piano - students
while away time in a cool refuge.

Hand rolled cigarettes
fuel passionate political debate as
mis-matched plastic chairs rock
under the rise and fall of young voices
a quartet of opinion
in a song of revolution
all black and white.

We sip Coca-Cola in the shade as
dark eyed men in ice cream jackets
lean lazily against the wooden bar
unfamiliar liquids in their cocktail glasses
traffic rolls past languidly
stirs sleep-filled air then sighs
an old beggar slips through the shadows
quietly gathers tips left unattended.

African Sunday

Kali sways along the path
head held high
a sun bright yellow dress
wrapped round her form

as if the fabric knew
her curves before
the seamstress cut and stitched
each tuck and tie.

Black curly hair piled high
on her head
with pins and combs
of tortoiseshell and bone

that fix her locks
though some escape
and frame her face
like silken thread.

Those bare black feet
often trudge that path of sand
as she carries pails of water
in each hand.

Russian Winter

Irina comes from Moscow

she knows about the way snow

falls layer upon chilled layer

meets the sky   wraps the city

sighs of despair unheard

women and men in skins and furs

hunker down

as words freeze on breath

moon's wide gape stares in silence

watching for the gaze of snowdrops

FRAGMENTS OF HISTORY

Tommy

He passed our house several times a day
steel tipped clogs clinking on the metalled road
long slow strides carrying his thin frame at an angle
head bowed like a meditating monk.
He looked so old we felt we couldn't count his years
parched skin stretched over sharp boned cheeks
blue-black shadows under cavernous eyes.

We stood pressed to the wall as he passed
not daring to breathe or speak
in case he turned his head to look at us,
the pungent smell shadowing him
wrinkled our noses but we stood stock still
we knew he slept in a corrugated barn
with his cow and dog for warmth.

Some days he drove the cow up the road,
often he carried a bale of hay on his back
his bony shoulders and legs wrapped
in rough sacking tied with baler twine.
They said he kept money under the straw
he marked the seasons through our childhood
I can't remember when we stopped noticing him.

Rose-hip Syrup

We all gathered rose-hips,
it was that time of year
when you wore your new
hand-knitted jumper, spent
Sunday afternoon walking up the lanes
with a paper bag from the pantry.

We all scoured the hedgerows for
oval orange hips, not juicy but soft
small enough to fit a child's fingers.
We all collected enough to fill a bag or two
to take to school on Monday morning,
at four pence a pound that was pocket money.

    Jack was different,
he collected them in sackfuls,
bulging black hessian tied with baler twine
carried on a plank nailed to old pram wheels.
His arms were scratched raw but we all
watched admiringly from the window
      we didn't understand.

Dancer

Dance for daddy he said
in the bright noisy bar,
so tapping her toes
she twirled on the table
in a pale pink cotton dress,
coins landed at her feet.

Another round landlord, he shouted
smiling at the assembled crowd
I'm thirsty Daddy she whispered,
run home to your mother he snarled,
as the pub door slammed

       silence
          and loneliness
              enveloped her.

Turpentine & Beeswax

Your tall frame bent over the bench
the tip of your tongue between your teeth
time meant nothing, dovetails and dowels
were fashioned with care, sharp chisels
shaped gentle curves across the grain
releasing the inner pattern of waves.

Smokey warmth from the iron range
carried the spicy smell of wood
through the oak-beamed rooms
of the old cottage cellar
oak sawn from trees that had
given way to age many years ago.

Outside a wool-white sky lay over hills
filled the wood with shifting mist
hung crystal drops on the cherry tree
as we drank sweetened tea from mugs
placed teacake dough in the bread oven
in memory of my grandmother.

Workbench and wood gone long ago
I lift the old tool bag from its rusty hook
carefully wrap each implement
in its own soft cloth, lay them in the bag
the old smell of turpentine and beeswax
turn the dusty air to remembered perfume.

The Shift of Time

We sidle down the main street
strut mascara and mini skirts
too old for the playground
too young for the pub

impatience thrums through our bodies
as the clock in the tower ticks
away the minutes too slowly
in our need to be grown up

we make do with a game of table tennis
rivalry runs through every move
as we tack to and fro either side of the table
one eye on the ball   the other on the boys

we drift back along the lane
stop to watch a game of bowls
laugh in the certainty that we
will never be so slow   so bent   so old

as if to prove this we run
to sit on the fish shop wall
share a portion of chips and watch
ghosts emerge from the works van

diatomite dust on each tired face
white dynamite in weary lungs
widows in waiting make cups of tea
for men already in decline

It Felt Like Plague

Just another school day
taking the register - *Sandra*
she's not here Miss
got summer flu
that's what our mothers told us.

An ambulance was called
we heard the words
iron lung - fear bred fury
    - don't share pencils
    - come straight home
    - wash your hands again.

Mothers weep   doors bang
the doctor doesn't sleep
suspicion swirls like chaff down streets
    - it breeds in dirty houses
    - he'd been swimming in the river
    - the gypsies were here last month.

A village held its breath
watching - waiting
for the heat to die down
for the virus to leave
calliper, paralysis, polio
new words in our vocabulary.

Friday

The sound of gunshot
cut through the valley mist
she stood in the kitchen
kneading dough for scones
the back door open a little
to let out the heat.
Her older children gone
to their own lives
her youngest out on the hill
rabbiting with his terrier
he'd be hungry later

April brought a breath of warmth
filling the village with promise
children's voices laughing
in the school playground
raised her spirits and so
she sang as the scones baked
swept the floor, set the table
and put the kettle on
just as the phone rang
clouds covered the sun.

The Sweetest Years

Ink stained desks in a stuffy classroom
skirts to our knees, jumpers rough
made us yearn for high heels
cotton dresses   red lipstick
Bardot sweaters
in hues of blue or pink

      we ran in corridors
         played hooky in games
      revised together
         in and out of school
      enough to pass exams
         jobs were easy come by
      boyfriends sent letters
         with ribbons tied round

we both fell in love   drifted out
shifted like Morecambe Bay sand
as we got it wrong   made it right
took the highs   shared the lows
hung on to our secrets   hid any doubts
miles between us deepened
we grew up   but not apart

Bags for Life

The bag with brass fastener
The bag for school lunch
The bag for my homework
The bag with blue canvas straps
The bag hidden for elicit make up
The bag for dad's fishing tackle
The bag with a pocket for hamsters
The fold-away bag for carrying shopping
The bag on the push-chair for nappies
The plastic bag for dirty washing
The bag with diamanté clasp
The bag with fake Gucci label
The bag made from cork
The bag you bought for my birthday
The bag made from palm leaves
The bag with pebbles from far away beaches
The bag for growing tomatoes
The bag for holding secateurs
The fabric bag for nurturing precious seeds
The big red bag filled with Christmas gifts
The bag you borrowed, it never came back
The bag I gave for charity
The bag that carries all I need

The Bevin Boy

All aboard, mind the gap

No choice but to go my love
through a November sky
in the middle of May
as a gust of steam from
the engine swirls
round my grey topcoat
on platform two
leaving you, sweetheart

I'll not wear khaki
as I play my part
called up to serve, not to fight
in a regiment, a foreign place
for my train runs north
from the cityscape
to deep seams of coal
in Durham mines

Rivers run
by the side of the track
fields of crops
to the horizon and back
give way to a skyline
of chimney stacks
blackened hills
all I can see

All change for Wearmouth colliery

Wagons clatter
as they haul the coal
red hot coke
runs down the ramp
the cage clangs shut
and we drop   a mile
where the air is thick
with a midnight dust

I dig for victory just like you
though my breath is short
my skin grained black
I crawl on my knees
my haul on the track
for rolling mills,
and coal-yards
fires and stoves

They call me coward
when I walk above
give me a white feather
as if I chose this life
swap a gun for a pick
for an easy time
would choking to death
repay my debt

Load the Kibble, turn the Windlass

Alternative

We thanked you
for your brilliant brain
Alan Turing OBE
you worked in code
to foil the Germans
saved our lives
to lose your own
to prejudice.

Castigated by the law,
how fickle now
the scorn you bore
branded as a criminal
loving in a different way
like many men
who lived in shadows
creeping round the edge.

A change of mind
a crime that never was
is now repealed by law,
we must apply for
permission to remove
your disgrace,
can suffering be
so easily erased.

They've rubber stamped
your pardon
flipped the coin -
guilty to innocent
who's to judge
so long in your grave
you'll never know.

Fabric of the Valley

It started when....

mist settled on the hillside
dripped from pine needles
seeped through the moss
trickled over rocks
with a quiet ticking
into the damp ravine

the water gathered
in the valley bottom
twisted it's way
to the outskirts of town
the locals named it
for the valley it ran through

workers used it in their efforts
to improve polyester yarn
damping, boiling for a long time
until the right texture was found
wonder fabric, fashion maker
came from the valley

....where the Crimple ran

Layering

It was a Sunday   which meant
nothing when the day was sweet
and the hedge needed laying
he held no truck with tractors
tearing tender spears raw   dripping sap
through spikes of twigs frayed like torn cloth.

He says the skill is in the eye
not in the strength of an arm
a cut in the right place laid to the sun
gives the pleacher new life to be
tomorrow's stem for flower and fruit
let wildlife pass through the smeuse.

The tools had been his fathers
each one hanging   oiled and sharp
on carefully aligned hooks in the shed
battle ready   glinting in the light
waiting for the heavy dew to lift
with the skylarks in early warmth.

He lays his hands gently along
the hawthorn trunk measuring
the right height to place the cut
the shape of his father's fingers
dented in the handle   the billhook
falls through the air   startling sparrows.

Lost Settlement at Kitridding

Deep down under my feet
the bones of the village lie quietly
sunk into the rich loam of the hillside
long forgotten names unbidden
by those who pass in a hurry.

West wind carries the song you sang
to your children cradled in sheepskin
sheltered from the ice sharp blast
long before wood was fashioned
nailed and painted for cots.

As winter sun breaches slate clouds
I think I glimpse your shadow foraging
for berries in the shrubs and bushes
filling skins with pure spring water
in ways you learned from your mother.

Needles on the trees rattle as if
disturbed by ghosts of hunters
running through the wolven forest
lit by a lazy fading moon
in pursuit of fleeing prey.

You are not meant to be seen
but remain hidden   potent
a link between history and present
revealing just a skeleton of stones
ritual patterns in hollows of earth.

Brigflatts

Holme Fell listens to
a madrigal from the Rawthey,
history woven through a hamlet
in ancient stones, plants, herbs

       place of peace and calm
       friendly silence fills spaces
       like the scent of blossom

Blood red flowers drip
over moss tipped tombstones
Isabella, Alice, Martha, Frances
shrouded in Queen Anne's Lace

       old and young lie together
       remembered in the tears of
       those left behind

Slated roof stuffed with moss
keeps snow from falling
on 'coal scuttle' bonnets
through winters sharp edge

       gentle creak of seasoned oak
       carved with commitment
       worn away by devotion

Sparrows and goldfinch
light as clear air
rest on ferns unfurling
by the mounting block

aroma filled hedgerows
a larder free for the taking
nourishment for every visitor

A Play in Three Acts

She knocks on our door
at the dead of night
in desperation coerces, persuades me
I am flattered, challenged,
decide to give it a go
reading, reciting in the bath, on the bus
in my lunch hour at school
after all the show must go on.

Chairs are set out   house lights are up
props acquired from shops and home
arranged on stage with hand-painted sets
costumes made by the undertaker's wife
skirts smoothed   deep breath
curtain up and into the swing
throw our voices   listen for a cue
search the audience for a friendly face

The after-show party runs late
into the night   with Babycham
vol-au-vents   pineapple on sticks
the greasepaint removed
we re-live every moment
glad we got through it   sad that it's over
weary now we set off for home
did someone mention next year

TRANSFORMED

Degeneration

she looked
  into the mirror
the middle
  of her face was
kaleidoscope - in grey
  she moved her head
up then down
  her face came in
and out of focus
  how could she
apply make up now
  her fingers traced
her eyelid as
  the black pencil
followed slowly
  seventy years of
easy beauty
  now a daily
challenge

Adrift

We never said goodbye
my mother and I
we travel in the ambulance
holding hands   making plans
talk of tomorrow
we both know this is not
the way it will be
I listen to calm voices
of paramedics   reassuring
and I look out of the window
at grey light and bare trees
the very depth of winter.

The hospital bed is too big
the bedclothes too flimsy
I slide my hand under the sheet
so your warm fingers
as light as a bird's wing
can rest untroubled in mine
I tell you the things we are doing
the bustle of our lives
whilst you lie silent   undecided
your breath is light as thistledown
slow as dreams
and I am adrift.

Packing Up

Yes that is my suitcase by the door
destination written loudly on the label
sadness
            shaken out then neatly folded
slipped tightly in-between my cotton shirts
feelings pressed
           flattened and zipped
into my wash bag with soothing creams
a growing sense of loss
           twisted in pink tissue
tucked into my shoes with woolly socks
a winter coat
         I'll wear my mac
with hankie in the pocket
memories begin to disintegrate
like the tickets
           curled within my sweaty hands
the straps hold down a rising breath of anger
as defiance presses up against the lid
suitcase firmly locked
        the travelling begins

I Took Your Name

......for a while it sits like
a pebble in my hand
unfamiliar but a comfort to hold
as the world around me
spins like a carousel

I think it changes me   moves me
to a place where others look at me
and say   she belongs   she conforms
fits in with the rest of us
so it makes them comfortable
easy in my company

With time it sidles into shape
as a whole name I recognise
without a twinge of loss
a drift from the past -
when we give it to our child
I take possession

Hand it over easily to doctors
teachers   girls in shops as if
it had always been mine
I have grown to fit the shape of it
slid into the hierarchy of women
who carried the name before

Our daughter keeps this name
passes it to her girls

Charades

We were never still
never quiet
conversations started by one
finished by the other
interrupted
never quite completed
but always laughing
through the school run
shopping   cricket teas
even when you moved away

Now the distance is a chasm
suspended in silence
fear in your eyes
 as words jumble
earnestly from your lips
with no form
frustration in your stricken body
desperately fighting
to move words from your head
to your mouth   to me

How can I translate
the monotone sound
filled with desperation
will the long game we play
bring understanding
across this chasm
wider than I can measure
though I can watch your face
hold your hand
bring you tea

Wide Eyes

The gathering crowd hesitate, anticipate
encouragement needed
to turn their heads his way

Forty minutes to sell his pitch
make his mark, earn his stars
on a teeming street in Edinburgh

He weighs the mood   spills words
pounces
        proffers danger
             breathes excitement
his life on the line for them

In no time he's up the ladder
balances astride the top rung
rides the cobbles to stay upright

He sheds his tee shirt   then his kilt
casts aside his   inhibitions
lost to the clapping of the crowd

I watch your face   you're mesmerised
fearful for his safety   unsure of the reaction
when he calls for   three sabres

the ladder walking
        sabre juggling
             hand clapping
all become one and you,
    you are hooked   smitten
engulfed   by festival fever

Lemon Drizzle

Fine white flour
    scoop by scoop
settles on metered scales

in a mixing bowl
    gram by gram
she measures deep yellow butter
bent at the edge
sliding into a mist of sugar

bamboo spoon

large eggs   bottle separated
yolks melded
whites whisked
lovingly made creamy by twists
turns   of a metal spoon
butter-greased tin

spare finger-full licked
from the side of the bowl

ovens warmth pushes back
the grey day's melancholy
lemon juice and sugar turn crisp crunchy

a pot of tea

Dry Eyed Grief

Followed the coffin, head bowed
as was expected
dressed in black, not my colour
your mate touches my arm, I flinch,
you're doing great love, he says
I'm not his love, not any man's love.

Blues music haunts the dusty air
black and blues I call it
I feel the burn of mourners' eyes
they know the score and pity me
but death makes a saint of any man.

The vicar starts to pray, I drift,
think of forty years ago,
you in winkle pickers, me in red lipstick
I remember it snowed, you fell, I laughed
you pushed me - hard   that was the start.

Your best friend stands to eulogise
about this man, father, husband -
what does he know, he's on your side
I fold my hands, breathe the spicy air
I cannot weep, I have no more tears.

Lent Lilies

You brought me flowers
yellow trumpets in a pale halo
bought on Saturday
given on Sunday
wet tissue round the stems
    I hadn't expected them

you were nine
all smiles and energy
living in the moment
coping with the changes
caused by my arrival
      brought me daffodils

I found a white jug
wiped my eyes as I filled it
hugged you as I put them
in the middle of the table
you bought two bunches
      gave one of them to me

Maryam's Song

She goes to the souq, mosque and hammam
like her mother, grandmother and many before
she's proud of her family, scared for her children
as the sound of tanks rumble past her door

where bombs reign and bombs rain down
children run through the streets

Car bombs blast through lives and houses
dust clouds mask the sun, young men all cough
destruction everywhere, families homeless
generations blown apart, no home shell proof

where bombs reign and bombs rain down
children cower in the streets

She leaves her home, just a pile of rubble
with her man, children, the clothes they wear
her heart breaks as she abandons her homeland
trudges on through hunger and loss in despair

where bombs reign and bombs rain down
children cry in the streets

Between her and a place of warmth and safety
the hungry sea roils from shore to shore
waves creep up the sand, fingers clawing
as the depth of the ocean calls for more

where bombs reign and bombs rain down
children lie in the streets

And bombs reign and bombs rain down
there are no more children in the streets

Why

1.

You
gave him
the rifle
and the training
why then are you so surprised when he shoots

2.

He
is a
peaceful boy,
his friends all said
plays dominoes at the local Shisha
He
has no
family here
foster parents
will care for him until he is eighteen
So
why would
five people
gang up on him
fracturing his skull, damaging his brain.
Kurdish community   saddened by this
want to avoid
culture of
revenge
here

Horse Power - Haiku

Sling-backed grey tacked horse
steps over the tall grass breathing
 in the cold spring air

                    Soft-lipped long-lashed eyes,
                    your friendly face searches mine
                    for signs of my love

Docile before the
farrier's large frame you lift
your feet for fitting

                    Wild eyes and raised mane
                    stare over the stable door
                    as if to say, you're late.

Short-legged scruffy brown coat
out in all weather fell ponies
stand together in wind.

                    Your pure chestnut brown
                    hunter clipped and shining coat
                    expects compliments

Cast clay makes soldiers
going nowhere beneath earth
guards emperor Chin

                    Slips slowly to earth
                    a soft tongue licks your body
                    stirs life, giving love

City Nights

marmalade and black cat
hunt with the rat pack
footprints in the snow cat
sneaking down the alley

catching mice and rats cat
trotting on the wall cat
landing on the dustbin
a 'steel-band' playing tabby

house cat or wild cat
living off their wits cat
purr at city fat-cats
licking up the cream

filing down his claws cat
to hangout with the cool cats
tripping down the bus track
street lights make him mean

siamese la-di-da cat
scoffs at raggy pole cat
scrapping with a persian
caterwaul resounds

singing with the tom cats
sniffing out a queen cat
slinking back at dawn cat
the milkman's on his rounds

Midsummer

Long awaited day
dawns with a turquoise sky
over a calm lake

Honeysuckle's heady scent
overwhelms the small garden

A pram stands in shade
netted to protect the babe
kicking sturdy legs

Washing hangs on the grey line
pegs bought from passing gypsies

Bread rises slowly
fills the air with heady yeast
smell of contentment

Distant siren breaks her reverie
not all the world is at peace

Roses snag her skirt
she picks them for the table
he will be home tonight

The shortest night of the year
when it seems a waste to sleep

Cuckoo calling from afar
won't see her young again
fostered out to a stranger

Shadows lengthen as the gate
swings open on its hinges

In the Ring

It's a mental game as you raise your glove
there's no room for fear, feel the strength
of the smell of rust in another man's blood

No limits, no stopping, is it like love
as you feel his force when your bodies clinch
in a mental game as you raise your glove

The cut on his eye oozing a warm flood
makes cold sweat on your brow, you inhale breath
with an odour of rust from this man's blood

Fist in, jabbing thrust, shoulders meet and shove
feet dance to and fro, a quick-fire agile path
in a mental game as you raise your glove

Bell rings, a moments rest, water tastes good
to a poser drowning the acid in his mouth
from a stench of rust in another man's blood

You just have to stay and take the beating
no half measures, gladiators meeting
in a mental game as you raise your glove
to the smell of rust, it's another man's blood

The Last Mile

Rarely a whole route walked in step
one stride longer, slower, steadier
the other pushing on up hills
to prove it can be done.

Sea-slapped coastline dips and rises
in harmony with gulls and gannets
oil tankers move slowly in the distance
to slip over the horizon with ease.

Unforgiving east wind scours the cliff
peels away clover and tormentil
to reveal ammonites held in ironstone
life lost in prehistoric days.

The bearing changes with every storm
paths give way to skeletons and fossils
a wavering fence all there is
as we breathe the salt spit air.

How far does our minds eye see
memories at our back push us forward
keep our balance on unsteady ways
when the tide pulls the moon from sleep

We reach the sift of bone-white pebbles
shed heavy boots to wade in waves
cool water sucking sweat from our limbs
walk the last mile together.

Watch me

Watch me change my mind

    in a flash   in an hour

in an everlasting beat of time

    as the moon rises   sets

pulled by wind

                  driven like rain

swept away in water   as a leaf

    at the joining of rivers

you think my course is clear

watch me change my mind

Acknowledgements

The following poems have appeared previously in other publications:

I Took Your Name, published in Speakeasy Magazine by Caldew Press, 2019.

The Shift of Time, first published in Speakeasy Magazine by Caldew Press, 2019.

Tommy, first published in Write on the Farm by Harestones Press, 2015, and subsequently in Persona Non Grata by Fly on the Wall Poetry Press, 2018.

Layering, first published in This Place I Know by Handstand Press, 2018, and subsequently together with **Lost Settlement at Kitridding; In the Ring; Charades; Samba Cafe, Lisbon; Packing Up; The Shift of Time** in Oak Tree Alchemy, Coverstory Books, 2019

Staffa Harp was written at a Poetry and Harp workshop in response to a piece of music about the Scottish Isles played by Christine Cochrane. It was published in the magazine, Poetry Scotland.

Reflections on Coniston were written on the Steam Gondola and recorded for the National Trust.

Bevin Boy was written and set to music in collaboration with Tom Crathorne, composer, and performed at the International Leeds Lieder Festival by William Kyle.

Russian Winter refers to 'snowdrops' which in this context is the Russian expression for homeless people who freeze to death on the streets.

Dry-Eyed Grief was written in response to an article in the Guardian about abused women.

In the Ring was written as a response to the comment by Chris Eubank "You just have to stay and take the beating".

Thank you to Geraldine Green, Jane Merritt and members of the Write on the Farm Group in Cumbria for a peaceful environment, friendship, encouragement and new ideas, some of which have grown into poems included in this book.

I also owe thanks to Brian Clark, David Smith and members of the North Yorkshire Stanza Group who have commented on and critiqued many of these poems to their benefit.

Thank you to my friends in Ripon Writers Poetry Group for their encouragement, particularly the late David McAndrew for his knowledgeable advice.

Thank you to the members of Skell Scriveners writing group for their support and advice.

My friend, Dorothy Brown, has read my poems avidly from the beginning, thank you.

Thank you to Malcolm Swann who spent his holiday designing the front cover for the book. A special thank you to my husband, David, for his support in all my poetic ventures.

Lightning Source UK Ltd.
Milton Keynes UK
UKHW022158260719
346886UK00013B/288/P